WARTI
CHILDHOOD

Mike Brown

SHIRE PUBLICATIONS

First published in Great Britain in 2009 by Shire Publications Ltd, Midland House, West Way, Botley, Oxford OX2 0PH, United Kingdom.
443 Park Avenue South, New York, NY 10016, USA.

E-mail: shire@shirebooks.co.uk   www.shirebooks.co.uk

A CIP catalogue record for this book is available from the British Library.

Shire Library no. 567   •   ISBN-978 0 7478 0737 7

Mike Brown has asserted his right under the Copyright, Designs and Patents Act, 1988, to be identified as the author of this book.

Designed by Ken Vail Graphic Design, Cambridge, UK and Typeset in Perpetua and Gill Sans.
Originated by PDQ Digital Media Solutions
Printed in China through Worldprint Ltd.

09 10 11 12 13   10 9 8 7 6 5 4 3 2 1

COVER IMAGE
1939 – war has broken out and Terrence John Harvey stands guard over the family Anderson shelter, with pop-gun, child's tin helmet and side cap. (Courtesy Mrs Pat Harris [nee Harvey])

TITLE PAGE IMAGE
A very young ARP Messenger, sporting his official ARP badge and 'M' ('messenger') helmet. (IWM D 3285)

CONTENTS PAGE IMAGE
Blackout cards. Card games and board games became very popular with the advent of the blackout, and the Blitz. With families spending hours stuck in the shelter, keeping the children entertained was a necessity.

ACKNOWLEDGEMENTS
I would like to thank the people who have allowed me to use illustrations, which are acknowledged as follows:

Peter Doyle, pages 3, 34 (upper), 51 (upper), and 51 (lower); Lewisham Local History Centre, page 9 (lower); Josie Simmons, page 55. All other illustrations are from the author's collection, or are credited within the captions as HMSO (Her Majesty's Stationery Office), or to the Imperial War Museum (IWM), followed by the photograph's reference number.

IMPERIAL WAR MUSEUM COLLECTIONS
Several of the photos in this book come from the Imperial War Museum's huge collections, which cover all aspects of conflict involving Britain and the Commonwealth since the start of the twentieth century. These rich resources are available online to search, browse and buy at www.iwmcollections.org.uk. In addition to Collections Online, you can visit the Visitor Rooms where you can explore over 8 million photographs, thousands of hours of moving images, the largest sound archive of its kind in the world, thousands of diaries and letters written by people in wartime, and a huge reference library. To make an appointment, call (020) 7416 5320, or e-mail mail@iwm.org.uk. Imperial War Museum www.iwm.org.uk

Shire Publications is supporting the Woodland Trust, the UK's leading woodland conservation charity, by funding the dedication of trees.

CONTENTS

INTRODUCTION

WHEN war broke out in September 1939, most British children were unprepared for it. Gas masks had been issued to the general public a year earlier, at the time of the Munich crisis, when there had also been evacuation practices at many inner-city schools, but on the whole, little had been done to prepare Britain's children for the coming war.

On the other hand, in Germany, the Hitler Youth had been proclaimed an official Government organisation in April 1933, just a few months after the Nazis had taken over; all other youth movements were either incorporated into it, or disbanded. All youngsters of suitable Aryan background were encouraged to join the movement.

Britain was about to experience nearly six years of total war, and caught in the middle of all this would be the children. They would be uprooted from all that was familiar to them as over two million were evacuated. Others would face their families being broken up as their fathers and older brothers were called up, and, later, their older sisters too. Worst of all, they would face death as first bombs and shells, and later 'flying bombs' and rockets, fell from the sky on homes and schools. Meanwhile along the way they would endure the privations of rationing, a fractured education and an uncertain future.

Yet Britain's youth were not merely passive victims; they would in their own way fight back, 'digging for victory', collecting salvage, acting as runners for the ARP (Air Raid Precautions) and the Fire Brigade, and in a thousand other ways. This is their story.

Opposite: Evacuee boys' 'Home Guard', with home-made guns. Just as in the real thing, the boy in charge gets the best equipment, in this case the helmet.

Below: Strube cartoon from January 1934 showing a Nazi 'Pied Piper' leading German children – his destination is indicated by the gas mask he carries and the bayonet in his hat instead of a feather.

THE CRAZY PIPER

The glories of war are now being taught to German school-children.

January 20th, 1934.

SCHOOL

EVACUATION

Long before war broke out it had been decided that the evacuation of children from what were seen as danger areas would best be carried out school by school. There were many advantages to the idea: children would be with their friends under the charge of people who were used to organising children, and whom the children would naturally trust and obey – their teachers, who would be evacuated with them. When they arrived at their destinations their education would have to be organised, and this would be done with the minimum of disruption if they were being moved as an educational 'unit'. Last, evacuation was not compulsory, and the Government worked hard to persuade people to send their children away; what better way to do so than for the children themselves to want to go, and if your school-friends were all going together, it was a great enticement for you to want to go with them.

There was one exception to the rule of evacuation by school: in order to keep brothers and sisters together younger siblings could go with the oldest child's school, although they would not always be billeted together at the other end.

In some cases suitable buildings were found to act as a temporary school: country houses whose owners had offered the buildings to the Government, or who had gone abroad (usually to America) to find safety, and whose houses had been requisitioned for war use. In preparation for war, many boarding schools had twinned with other such schools in safe areas. Once war broke out they moved in together, sharing dormitories and classrooms. There were also the Camp Boarding Schools. Early in 1939 the Government had passed the Camps Act, which planned to set up around fifty camps in the country. These were to act as holiday camps for 350 children each in peacetime, and evacuation schools, each housing about 250 pupils and staff, in a war. In the event, thirty-one of these camp boarding schools were constructed, the first being completed early in 1940, and by the middle of 1941, thirty of the camps were in use, housing over 6,000 children in all. They had wooden

Opposite:
A reading lesson
taking place in the
air raid shelter
of Creek Road
School in
Deptford.
(IWM D 3161)

7

Evacuees on a train, wearing their school labels and carrying gas masks. (HMSO)

buildings in which, as well as the normal subjects, gardening, pig- and poultry-keeping, shoe repair and house management were taught.

Sometimes abandoned churches or farm sheds were put to use, especially for small primary schools, but on the whole, especially for bigger schools, the evacuated school shared buildings with an existing school in the reception area, with one school using it in the morning, and the other in the afternoon. In many areas hostels providing private study facilities were set up for senior pupils, and evacuation hostels for younger children, but the vast majority of pupils shared the local school and were billeted in private homes.

A London school evacuation group. Note the banner and the teacher's armbands; this number would also be on the children's labels.

AIR RAID SHELTERS AND GAS MASK DRILLS

With war approaching the Government pressed on with building air raid shelters in schools, but by the outbreak of war this had not been completed in all schools. The Government leaflet *War Emergency Information and Instructions*, issued as soon as war broke out, contained the following: 'All day schools are to be closed for instruction for one week from today.

Subsequent re-opening will rest with the authorities of the schools and will be announced locally.' Children were only allowed back when air raid shelters had been provided, so many children had a surprise extra few weeks' holiday that September as work was hurriedly completed. Sometimes temporary classes were arranged in various churches and halls where small groups of children attended at set times to be given work to do at home. Once the shelters were complete, life more or less returned to normal, except in the evacuation areas. Here many schools were kept closed for longer, to encourage parents to send their children away.

In the inner cities, many schools had few children left, and no teachers, as these had all gone with the schools. School buildings were taken over as auxiliary fire stations, rescue party depots or ambulance stations. As increasing numbers of evacuees returned, education authorities gave in, and schools slowly re-opened, often continuing to share their premises with the ARP services who had moved in during their absence.

In schools the normal routine now included gas mask drill, where the children, on a given signal, would put on their gas masks, and carry on working with them on. This was not only a drill, but to get the children used to wearing them. Air raid shelter drills also took place fairly regularly, rather like fire drills today. Again at a given signal the children would file out to their allotted place; in most schools there would be several small shelters.

A boy on his way to school, asking a variation of the wartime slogan 'Is Your Journey Really Necessary?'

Left: Young evacuees playing 'Oranges and Lemons'. The woman on the far right wears Women's Voluntary Service uniform: the WVS played a significant part in running evacuation hostels.
(IWM D 743)

School premises were often shared with civil defence groups. Here a school in Lewisham is also being used as a Stretcher Party depot.

9

Gas mask drills were a regular feature of wartime schooling. Note the various gas mask cases, including the issue cardboard boxes, carried by the children.
(IWM D 3162)

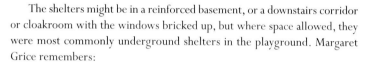

Nursery children entering a typical underground school air raid shelter. Practice drills such as this were regularly carried out, much as fire drills are today.

The shelters might be in a reinforced basement, or a downstairs corridor or cloakroom with the windows bricked up, but where space allowed, they were most commonly underground shelters in the playground. Margaret Grice remembers:

> Our school shelter was made of concrete sunk into the ground. We had air raid drill; teacher would blow her whistle and we would stand up by our desks, then walk in orderly lines to cloakrooms, get our gasmasks and coats, then walk to the shelter, still in lines. When you entered the shelter there were steps to go down, then you would proceed up and down the benches in a snake like procession filling the seats in turn. We then put our gas masks on; we would sit still until the teacher blew her whistle, we would take our gas masks off then we would stand and climb out of the shelter; orderly fashion again. There was no pushing, shoving or running; this rule was instilled into us.

As the Blitz began, these practices became the real thing. Teachers worked hard to keep the children calm in what could be very fraught times. Knitting was encouraged amongst the girls, and singing was popular, as the noise drowned out the sounds of battle outside – several schools set up a piano in the shelter! Another way of drowning out the noise was to chant the times tables.

THE BLITZ

In Kent, with the Battle of Britain raging overhead, it was not only bombs that fell: empty bullet cases, and parts of aircraft also came down. One ex-pupil of Maidstone Grammar School remembered a period when the boys had to go over every foot of their football pitch before each game in order to clear it of splinters.

Inevitably schools were hit, sometimes with horrible casualties, such as one boys' school at Petworth, which suffered thirty-one fatal casualties, and Sandhurst Road School in southeast London, where thirty-eight children and six teachers were killed. Thankfully, most raiding took place at night, so when schools were hit there were no children in them. In London 150 schools were destroyed and over 200 damaged, mostly with no casualties. Mrs Freddie Venables remembers: 'One night our school had the central part blown out and we were joyfully sent home while the damage was patched up. We spent our gym and games periods filling in the bomb craters on the playing fields.'

Children arriving at Moorside Road School to find their school a victim of the Blitz. How upset they are by the news can be seen on their faces.
(IWM D 3175)

And Peggy Hoare recalls:

In March 1945, on alighting from a bus for the ten-minute walk to our secondary school, we began to notice an increasing number of broken windows. When we reached school it seemed to be all right until we saw that all the glass had gone. During the night a V2 had landed in the park which adjoined our playing field. We were allowed to go to our form rooms in small, supervised groups to collect personal things, then we had an unexpectedly long Easter holiday.

When this happened schools would be shared. Pam Cleverly remembers that in 1942 in one raid on Canterbury her school was destroyed. 'For the first term we shared the boys' school building which was untouched. One week we went from 9 am until 1 pm and the next week from 1 pm to 5 pm.' More often teachers would go several times a week to pupils' houses where they would teach small groups of similar-aged children, until places could be found for the pupils in other schools.

In 1943 'tip and run' raids (sudden attacks by low-flying fighter-bombers) became common. These raids usually took place during the day, putting schools into the front line again. A further danger arose in that these raids often occurred without the air raid warning being sounded, as happened at Sandhurst Road School. Air raid drills took on

Life goes on – children play around a bomb crater in the playground of Lombard Road School.
(IWM D 3170)

A class being taught by their teacher, who is wearing his Home Guard uniform.

School children sorting salvage in their school hall. Note the many German incendiary bomb fins in front of the centre group of girls – everything could be used for salvage. (IWM D 3166)

a new urgency: they meant not only going to the shelters, but at a different signal, ducking under your desk to take immediate cover. In the following year the threat changed to V1s and V2s. Again the warning time was minimal, and in the areas of greatest danger schools were supplied with Morrison shelters to be placed inside the smaller classrooms, or Andersons to be put up just outside entrances or close to classroom walls.

With the V1s, many schools in the danger areas used older pupils as raid spotters. Sitting at a desk outside the school, they would look out for V1s heading towards the school. On seeing one they would sound the alarm, giving the others a chance to duck under the table or into the shelter.

In boarding and secondary schools, older pupils often became members of fire watching parties, taking it in turns to do duty, usually on the school roof, watching for incendiary bombs, armed with buckets of sand and stirrup pumps.

Children raising money for 'War Weapons Week'. Note the anti-blast tape on the windows to prevent flying glass.
(IWM D 5022)

THE WAR EFFORT

Schools did their bit towards the war effort. Salvage collections were common, with schools in the same area competing to collect the most paper, rags and so on, with the results being announced at the end of each term. Knitting 'comforts' for the troops was something girls, and sometimes boys, were encouraged to do, with schools adopting a ship or military unit, and knitting clothes and blankets for them, and also sending letters, books and magazines to their adopted units.

Schools set up victory gardens, or even allotments, and growing food to be used in the school kitchens became a timetabled lesson. Most schools set up National Savings Groups where children would buy savings stamps to pay for the war; they would also collect money for the local Spitfire Fund (to buy a Spitfire), or for 'Warship Week', 'Salute the Soldier Week', and so on.

SCHOOL MILK AND SCHOOL DINNERS

School dinners, not always provided before the war when most children went home for lunch, became almost universal, as many mothers found work in munitions or other factories. In 1942, the Government started the School Milk Scheme: children – over 3.5 million of whom already received free or cheap milk – now were given half a pint a day in school, as well as cod liver oil.

UNIFORM

As with everything else, shortages affected schools. The most basic materials – pencils, paper, books – became shortage items. Clothes quickly became a real problem, especially in 1942 with the introduction of clothes rationing. In many schools the uniform was relaxed, or dropped altogether, although one or two of the more traditional public and grammar schools continued to insist on full uniform, which often needed all a child's coupons.

Right: An advertisement for Bird's custard from January 1945, showing a girl wearing a gym slip. The gym slip in school colours was the standard uniform for secondary schoolgirls throughout this period.

Below: A Government 'Make-do and Mend' advertisement – Judy's new school frock. At a time of clothing rationing, many children were dressed in clothes made from out-worn items.

Below right: Pattern book. Knitting 'comforts' for the forces was encouraged amongst both boys and girls.

Still the Best!

BIRD'S CUSTARD

BIRD'S CUSTARD AND JELLIES

ISSUED BY THE BOARD OF TRADE

8 COUPONS SAVED

-and it all started with two old coats!

Here's Judy's new school frock, nearly finished. Mother made it from a serge coat Judy had worn two summers ago, plus her old flannel blazer. Mother really wasn't much of a dressmaker— but she went to a Make-do and Mend class where she got just the help she needed.

FROM THE BLAZER
Bodice top and sleeves were cut from this material after it had been unpicked and washed.

FROM THE COAT
Unpicking and pressing came first—then the skirt, belt, collar and cuffs were cut out.

PERHAPS YOU'RE AN EXPERT YOURSELF?

Then your help is badly needed by those not as clever with their needles. Give a hand to your next door neighbour or ask a local Women's Organisation how you can help them.

Knitting for the Service Girls

SPLENDID COMPETITION

YOU'VE knitted for soldiers, sailors, airmen and refugees, but what about the Service Girls ? You've not thought of them, perhaps, but we have, and find they want lots of things—things like ankle socks, gloves, scarves and pullovers. So get out your needles and start now.

The exciting part about this competition is that not only will a W.A.A.F., Wren, A.T.S. or Land Girl be having a much needed "woollie" gift from your fair hands, but you may win something for yourself, for we are offering

30 Marvellous Book Prizes

for the best knitted garments. No garments will be returned, but after the competition is over they will be presented to Britain's Service Girls by the Duchess of Northumberland's Comforts Fund, who have kindly undertaken the work of distribution for us.

Your knitting should be in a suitable Service colour, but you may choose your own design. Fix your name, address, and age to your work and send to the EDITOR, "GIRL'S OWN PAPER," 4 Bouverie-street, London, E.C.4. Closing date MAY 27, 1941.

NOTE.—This competition is arranged for three months and prizes will be awarded each month. Thus slow knitters have a marvellous opportunity. So tell your friends.

RAIDS

GAS MASKS

Poison gas had been the terror weapon of the First World War, and in 1936, with war brewing, the British Government began to build up stocks of gas masks. It was found that the normal civilian mask, in a small size, was suitable for children above the age of five, but that a separate mask would be needed for children under five, as the shape of their faces was different. There would also need to be a mask for babies. Many designs were tried, including cardboard boxes fitted with pumps – a sort of oxygen tent – and a hood that could be attached to prams. By 1937, an anti-gas helmet for babies and children up to two years old had been developed, but there was still nothing for children between two and five.

The anti-gas helmet for babies was generally called the 'baby-bag' because most of the baby fitted inside it, while whoever was looking after the child pumped air in with a sort of bellows. The whole thing was heavy and unwieldy, especially as it would have to be carried whenever the baby was taken out of the house.

Respirators, as gas masks were officially called, were first issued at the time of the Munich crisis in September 1938. Fitting stations were hurriedly opened in schools, village and town halls. Unfortunately, the 1.5 million children's respirators and the 1.4 million baby bags that were needed were not yet available. After the crisis had passed it was decided to leave those masks that had been issued with the public, and to issue cardboard box carriers.

This, for many children, was the first sign that war was in the air, but for most, the mask was a thing of potential fun – rude noises could be made with them. Realising that children might abuse their masks, many parents locked them away after the crisis, as this excerpt from *William and ARP*, published in 1939, shows:

'What do they [ARP] do, anyway?' demanded Douglas.
'They have a jolly good time,' said William vaguely. 'Smellin' gases an''

Opposite:
Children entering an Anderson shelter. The boy is, quite correctly, carrying his gas mask. The Anderson had to be erected in a hole dug several feet into the ground, which is why they need to step down onto the chair.
(IWM D 778)

Right: A girl showing her school chums some shrapnel in the playground. Notice their gas mask bags, and the 'pixie hood' of the girl third from the left – popular headwear for younger girls. (IWM D 3166)

Above: An almost nightmarish scene, yet it actually shows a nurse wearing her gas mask, carrying a baby in the baby's gas helmet, or 'baby-bag' as they were widely known. (IWM D 648)

bandagin' each other an' tryin' on their gas masks. I bet they bounce out at each other in their gas masks, givin' each other frights. I've thought of lots of games you could play with gas masks, but no one'll let me try. They keep mine locked up. Lot of good it'll be in a war locked up where I can't get it. Huh!'

Right: Children's book Let's Play Firemen. That this is a wartime book is shown by the firemen's tin helmets.

By now a small child's mask was being rushed into production. Known to the public as the 'Mickey Mouse' or 'Donald Duck' mask, it was made in bright red and blue. Getting the average three-year-old to put on a gas mask could prove difficult, so the mask was made in these bright colours to make it look like a toy. Indeed the Government suggested that parents devise games involving putting on their masks, firstly so that children would not have hysterics on seeing their parents in a gas mask, and secondly as a sort of gas mask drill for the children.

A few weeks after war broke out, distribution of adult masks was complete; by late October, baby-bags also, and by the end of January 1940 the issue of children's masks was complete. They were issued in cardboard boxes, which soon fell to bits unless carefully treated, and few children did that. Indeed, as the quote from *William* demonstrated, gas masks made great playthings. They could be used as goalposts in a game of football, and in the absence of a ball, could be used as one. Another game was a variation on conkers, in which, holding the box by the carrying string, you took it in turns to bash each other's masks, until one box fell to bits. Even if you were not so violent with it, it was hard to keep the box from disintegrating. Many parents invested in gas mask cases, usually sold for about one to two shillings. There were many types of these, the most common being a sort of canvas bag for girls, and a metal tin, often cylindrical, for boys.

Left: Wartime teddy bear wearing the 'Mickey Mouse' gas mask. These were for children from about eighteen months to about five years old.

Below: Amidst the rubble of a bomb-strike a boy plants a Union Jack. Such patriotic displays, or signs chalked on the walls of bombed buildings, helped maintain morale amongst the ruins.
(IWM D 1303)

Child's identity card from 1943. These were used to claim new food and clothing ration books.

THE BLACKOUT

Another early defence measure was the blackout, brought in as soon as war broke out. Street lights were switched off, and from sunset to sunrise it was illegal to show any lights that were visible from the outside. From mid October 1939, people were allowed to use torches in the street if obscured by two layers of tissue paper, but they had to be put out once an air-raid warning was sounded. Cars and even bicycles had to have their headlights similarly obscured. The *Boy's Own Paper* of May 1940 told its readers:

Many readers must have found by now how difficult it is to obtain satisfactory results from makeshift shields for torches and cycle lamps. As a rule, if the mask is effective enough to satisfy ARP regulations it is seldom possible to see more than a yard or two with the illumination given. There is a new Lucas shield and a special battery lamp, however, that are both efficient and reliable. The Lucas 'Masklite' Cycle Headlamp Shield, which is patented and registered, consists of a mask obscuring the upper half of the front glass, and a shield round the underside of the bulb which renders the lower half of the reflector non-effective. The price is only 6d.'

To make driving in the blackout safer, kerbs were painted white, and white bands painted around obstacles such as trees, lamp-posts and pillar boxes. White lines were also painted down the middle of roads, a road safety measure that still exists today. In spite of all this, there was a steep rise in road deaths, especially of children; during the first four months of the war road deaths were more than double those of the same period in the previous year.

The Government brought in a speed limit of 20 mph in built-up areas during the blackout, while pedestrians were encouraged to wear something white, or carry a newspaper. All sorts of luminous items (very many of which didn't work) were on sale, including badges, buttons, glasses, and even dog leads.

Keeping oneself occupied during the long hours of the blackout was a theme of many advertisements, such as these from the spring of 1940.

CHEMISTRY EXPERIMENTS FOR BLACK-OUT EVENINGS

Post Free OFFER of SAMPLE PARCEL containing many useful pieces of

CHEMICAL APPARATUS 2/9

Write also for free PRICE LIST of other sets.

BECK (Scientific Dept. C), 60, High Street, Stoke Newington, London, N.16.
Booklet "Experiments in Chemistry" 6d. P.O.

SHELTERS

From 1938, for those who could afford it, builders offered to erect private shelters of varying quality in people's gardens. The Government provided 'Anderson' shelters to those who could not afford to buy shelters. The Anderson shelter was 6 feet high, 4 feet 6 inches wide, and 6 feet long, and was made of corrugated steel sheets. They were delivered in pieces, and householders were expected to erect them themselves, sinking them in a hole three feet deep. This was a job which the children could help with, though not always successfully, as Gordon Moore remembers: 'My dad had marked out where we were to dig, a hole six by six foot and two foot deep; Bernard swung his fork up in the air and drove it down right though my shoe, my foot, and skewered my foot to the ground.' If you were too old or frail to erect the shelter yourself, you might contact the local Boy Scouts to do it for you.

By the outbreak of war, almost 1.5 million Andersons had been distributed. This still meant that the majority of people had no

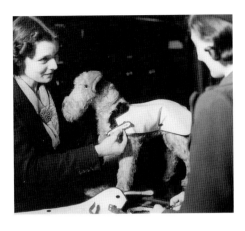

Darkness descended on the streets in the form of the blackout. All sorts of luminous devices went on sale, including this luminous dog's jacket. In reality few of these items were actually of any use.
(IWM D 66)

shelter; for them there might be public shelters available. Many of these were dark, damp, and definitely unhygienic – few had considered the need for toilets, and a bucket was often all that was provided. For this reason many people preferred to stay at home; for them there was the cellar, the cupboard under the stairs, or, if nothing else, huddling under the kitchen table.

Both Andersons and public shelters were designed around the idea that raids would be short and sharp when, as it turned out, raids often lasted several hours. Many hours were spent sitting cooped up in shelters when the warning sounded. Under these conditions children could easily get bored in a shelter; magazines suggested card games or board games to keep them occupied, while advertisers recommended their products 'for blackout evenings'. Books for children, with titles such as *The Shelter Fun Book* and

The Anderson shelter. Part of its strength lay in its being partially buried in the ground, and the earth from the hole piled on top of it, but this also led to its tendency to flood.

Mum, Dad and
their seven
children grab
a little sleep
in a public air raid
shelter. For those
children not
evacuated from
the towns and
cities, this was
a common
experience in the
early period of
the war.
(IWM D 1614)

The Blackout Book were popular, as they were full of quizzes, puzzles, stories and plays to be acted out.

As the autumn of 1940 moved into winter, the drawbacks of the Andersons became obvious. Firstly they were cold: many reported waking in the morning to find frost on the inside of the shelter. Official advice was to make a flowerpot heater: place one good-sized flowerpot the right way up. Inside this put a lighted candle, then place another flowerpot, upside down, on top of the first one, making sure the hole in the bottom (or top, as it now was) was not blocked. The heat from the candle would warm up the flowerpots, which would in turn keep the shelter warm throughout the night. The second and more difficult problem with the Anderson shelters was that, sunk down into the ground as they were, they had a tendency to flood, either because of a high ground water table, or because surface water would run in during a downpour. Often this would not be noticed until the family were driven by the warning siren into the shelter, only to find themselves up to their ankles in water.

In London, the Underground stations were used as public shelters. The great attraction for children in the public shelters was that there were usually other children there to play with, and often space for running around. The Underground had the added attractions of chocolate vending machines, escalators, and later, canteens, where drinks, sandwiches and buns could be bought. Also there were the trains themselves, and the braver, older children, would, unbeknown to their parents, travel around the tube, returning to their station and their family in time for bed.

In March 1941 a new indoor air raid shelter called the Morrison began to be provided by the Government, providing a bed for two adults and one child at night, and a table by day. They were erected in a downstairs room, and the shelter was used as a table during the day; photographs show children playing table tennis on them, using them as a stage for impromptu performances, or as a dining table.

Bernard Quinlan's father painted a map of Europe on the top of their Morrison: 'With our metal toy tanks, guns, soldiers, planes and ships, we carefully recreated the advance of the Germans, the evacuation from Dunkirk, the raids on St Nazaire and other targets, and the landings in Normandy.'

At night, however, many children slept in them as a matter of course, so that, in the event of the warning sounding, they would not even need to be woken. Sometimes the whole family slept in them, but more often Mum and Dad (if he were not in the forces) would sleep upstairs in their bed, or in times of heavy raiding, on top of the Morrison, going inside in response to the warning.

Many continued to use public shelters; some had no space for a Morrison, others preferred the feeling of security in being part of a large crowd, or the feeling of community. Here, not only were the sleeping and sanitary arrangements hugely improved, but entertainment began to be laid on. In smaller shelters sing songs were the order of the day, augmented by individual performances, often by the children. In larger shelters this was

Civil Defence workers, including a young messenger. Bombing would quickly bring down the telephone wires, so both boys and girls were enlisted into the Messenger service, carrying important messages by bicycle or on foot. (IWM D 7926)

The Morrison table shelter. This cartoon by Sillince draws the inevitable comparison between the shelter and a birdcage. They were, however, remarkably effective.

" By the way, did you remember to feed the canary?"

Weetabix advertisement from 1941 showing a child's tin helmet. There were several types of these on sale, most being more decorative than practical, yet they were, for boys especially, an object of great desire.

added to by concerts, and even plays, performed by ENSA (Entertainments National Service Association) or another such group. In Chislehurst Caves, for instance, where tens of thousands of southeast Londoners took shelter, there were two raised performance areas. And at Christmas, shelter parties for the children were arranged, although this sometimes led to fights as children who did not usually come to the shelter tried to gatecrash the party.

In the last year of the war came the V-weapons. These were Hitler's 'secret weapons', designed to pound Britain into submission. The V1, better known as the 'doodlebug', 'buzz-bomb', or 'flying bomb', was a rocket-propelled, unmanned aircraft. Children as well as adults soon learned to recognise the unmistakable noise of its engine, and to know that as long as you could hear it you were safe, throwing yourself to the ground when it cut out. They even devised little skipping rhymes like this one:

First you hear the engine,
Then you hear it stop,
Dive and count to thirty,
Then you can get up.

This is a very accurate description of a V1 strike; it would only come down when the engine cut out, when it would crash to the ground and explode. If you counted to thirty after the engine cut out, you were safe, as by then it had crashed and exploded.

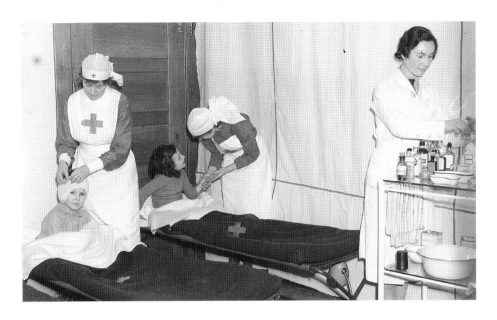

Above: Children in the first aid post of the air raid shelter of John Keeble Church. Whilst this is probably a posed shot, over 15,000 children under the age of 16 were killed, missing, or seriously wounded during the Blitz. (IWM D 1438)

Left: A group sitting down to a meal in the air raid shelter of John Keeble Church. Note that the children are enjoying a rare wartime treat – a real boiled egg! Under rationing adults received about three eggs a month. (IWM D 1436)

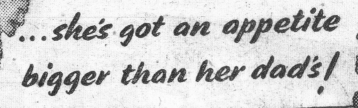

...she's got an appetite bigger than her dad's!

Girls and boys in their 'teens are, or should be, growing tremendously, and their bodies are *changing*, too. They really do need a lot of food — as much as father, or even more — especially the body-building foods; so allow for them when laying out your points.

The **midday meal** is particularly important. The "tea and bun" habit is very bad for them. If there is no canteen or suitable eating place near their work, put up packed meals. Sandwiches filled with cheese, scrambled dried egg, pilchard or spam and shredded raw vegetable and a milky drink, is a perfect "balanced" meal.

✶✶✶✶✶✶✶ Fitness for the 'teen ages ✶✶✶✶✶✶✶

RATIONS THE FOUNDATION. *The 'teen ages must have their full share of every single rationed food ; no poaching by other members of the family !* **MILK**. *It is most important that they get the priority milk allowed to children up to 18.*

Extra Body-builders

1. DRIED BEANS, PEAS AND LENTILS are cheap in cost and points, and high in building-value. To increase their value, serve them in dishes which contain a little meat, milk, dried egg or cheese. It is far better than using them alone.
2. GRADE 3 SALMON is by no means grade 3 in food value ! Put it high on your list.
3. CANNED PILCHARDS are also "tops" as builders.
4. FRESH FISH — HERRINGS are the best, when obtainable.
5. DRIED EGG is packed with the right nourishment ; take up all you can get.
6. HOUSEHOLD MILK, though it has no cream, is rich in muscle and bone-building nourishment. Use as much of it as you can get, in drinks, puddings, cakes, etc.

Vegetables are Vital

1. GREENS AND ROOT VEGETABLES are absolutely essential to make up necessary vitamins and mineral requirements. Not only health protection, but growth and development depend on them, to say nothing of good skins and clear complexions. Big helpings every day.
2. VEGETABLES should be shredded to aid quick cooking, and served at once — never "kept hot" or reheated.
3. VEGETABLE WATER should be used for soups or stews.
4. SALADS : "Something green and raw" every day should be a rule.

Best Energy Foods

1. BUTTER, MARGARINE AND COOKING FAT. Remember, full rations, please.
2. POTATOES ; in plenty, the best food to "fill up" on.
3. OATMEAL ; has body-building value as well as energy.
4. BREAD ; you want to cut down your household consumption of bread ; let the grown-ups and light workers do most in this respect.
5. SUGAR AND JAM are not so important ; but, of course, "fair shares" of these, too.

ISSUED BY THE MINISTRY OF FOOD (S63)

RATIONING

FROM the very beginning of the war, it was realised that one of Britain's greatest weaknesses was its need to import much of the raw materials needed to survive, especially food, wood, and oil. Petrol was rationed almost from the first, and in November it was announced that food would begin to be rationed from January 1940.

As a first step to introducing food rationing, every man, woman, and child in the country was registered on Friday 29 September 1939. Following this, everyone was issued with an identity card. The information gathered was then used to issue ration books in late October; these had a buff cover for those over six years old, and green for those under six.

Food rationing began on 9 January 1940; the first items to be rationed were butter and bacon at 4 ounces each a week per person, and sugar, at 12 ounces. These still had to be paid for, but as well as the money, you had to hand over your ration book, from which the appropriate coupons had to be cut out by the shopkeeper. (In 1941, to save the many hours spent cutting out coupons, shopkeepers were allowed to cross out or stamp coupons.)

The basic principle of rationing was 'fair shares for all': although of course there was some complaining, sometimes a lot, about the size of the ration, it was tempered by the thought that everyone got the same, with a few variations for younger children. As the war went on the list of rationed goods, as well as the amounts allowed, was ever changing – the first growing, the second usually shrinking.

In March 1940 meat was rationed, this time by value – 1s. 10d per week for those over six years old, children below that age receiving half that amount. 'Meat' did not include offal such as liver, kidneys and heart, and products such as meat pies, paste or sausages. Being coupon-free, these became sought after, and were often kept 'under the counter' for favoured customers.

People began to keep rabbits in their back gardens as a source of ration-free meat; they were easy to feed and look after, and made cute pets for the children to play with. But herein lay the problem: when the time came to kill them, many could not bring themselves to do so, and even if they could, there was

Opposite: Children received extra milk under the ration scheme, though this was sometimes shared amongst the whole family. The Ministry of Food worked hard to ensure that such extras went to those for whom they were meant.

At the end of September 1939, everyone had to be registered, so that they might be issued with identity cards and, subsequently, ration books. Here children examine their newly received documents. (IWM D 779)

Even though they received extra coupons, clothes rationing was particularly difficult for mothers of growing children, who not only wore out their clothes, but also, as this postcard shows, grew out of them.

GOD didn't know when he made us to grow— there'd be coupons!

often a tearful mealtime ahead, as the children refused to eat a beloved pet. Later, more exotic alternatives to meat appeared in the form of whale meat (almost universally hated), and horse flesh – many children were presented with this without their mother ever letting on what it was that they were eating.

In April Lord Woolton became the Minister of Food. He was determined that rationing should be more than just fair shares for all, and that Britain's children would receive the right diet to help them grow fit and strong. He became one of Churchill's most successful ministers; indeed, he was so personally associated with the distribution of food, that one little girl, reaching 'Give us this day our daily bread' in her prayers, asked her mother why we had to have both God and Lord Woolton.

As a result of Lord Woolton's plan, in July 1940 the National Milk Scheme was started. Under the scheme, children below the age of five, expectant and nursing mothers were supplied with a pint of milk a day, either free, or at 2d a pint if the family could afford it. What milk remained was shared amongst the rest of the nation, usually amounting to about three pints a week each. One of the less favourable consequences of this scheme from a child's point of view was that commercial production of ice cream was prohibited, and another peacetime treat disappeared.

Over the next months more and more items (such as onions) became almost impossible to get, or went 'on the ration', including tea, cooking fats, jam, marmalade, syrup and honey. Food, which has always been a major preoccupation for most children, became even more so. It wasn't that they did not get enough to eat, but what they did get was limited in scope, and therefore meals became somewhat monotonous.

A good example of this was the use of the potato; this was one food item that could be produced at home in bulk, and the Ministry of Food encouraged their consumption through 'Potato Pete', a cartoon character aimed especially at the children. Pete had his own recipe book, full of suggestions and recipes to make eating potatoes (yet again!) more varied, such as Fadge (Irish potato bread), potato cakes, potato pancakes, potato pastry, and so on.

Even potatoes were not to be wasted: they were to be cooked in their skins – never peeled. In December 1940, a Government 'Food Facts' advert contained the following poem:

Those who have the will to win
Eat potatoes in their skin,
Knowing that the sight of peelings
Deeply hurts Lord Woolton's feelings.

The size of the meat ration fell sharply, as a result of which fish became a popular alternative, and in its turn became short. To fill the gap, weird and wonderful new types of fish appeared including Icelandic salt cod and snook.

That May, the first consignment of 'Lend-Lease' food arrived in Britain from the USA, including cheese, canned foods and lard.

GOOD HOUSEKEEPING'S book of
CHILD FEEDING
IN WARTIME
6ᴰ

The Ministry of Food, and women's magazines provided recipes and tips for preparing satisfying meals with the limited materials provided under rationing, such as this booklet from *Good Housekeeping*.

Child's food ration book from 1942. These green-covered books were issued to children under six, who received less meat but extra milk and welfare foods, such as orange juice and cod liver oil.

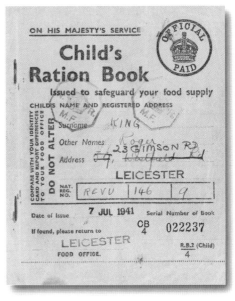

ON HIS MAJESTY'S SERVICE

Child's Ration Book

Issued to safeguard your food supply

CHILD'S NAME AND REGISTERED ADDRESS
Surname KING
Other Names Roger
Address 23 Gimson Rd,
LEICESTER
NAT. REG. NO. REVU 146 9
Date of Issue 7 JUL 1941   Serial Number of Book
If found, please return to CB 4 022237
LEICESTER
FOOD OFFICE.   R.B.I (Child) 4

Right: Potato Pete was used by the Ministry of Food to encourage the maximum consumption of potatoes instead of other, less plentiful but more interesting foods. His recipe book contained ideas to use potatoes in more varied ways.

Below: Sheet music for 'When can I have a banana again?' Imported fruit such as bananas, oranges and pineapples became little more than a memory, as this song from 1943 shows.

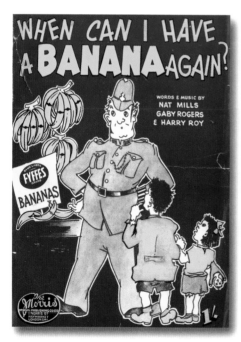

With these came new foods, such as soya flour (a sweet flour intended for cakes or biscuits) and – what was to become a favorite amongst many children – Spam ('shoulder of pork and ham', a canned, precooked meat product).

Fruit from abroad became scarce; at the end of September 1941 came the Orange Distribution Scheme, in which the number of oranges that a customer could buy at any time was limited to the equivalent of one pound in weight. However, for the first week that a retailer had any oranges, they were required to give priority to those with the green ration book, and to mark it to show each purchase – signs on fruit stalls stated 'Oranges for children only'. Of course it was unusual for a retailer to have any oranges anyway, while pineapples and bananas became almost mythical.

On 1 June 1941 the Government announced that clothes rationing would commence the following day. Each person would receive sixty-six coupons to last one year. In addition to this, everyone below the age of sixteen was issued a supplementary sheet of ten coupons, while some received an additional ten or twenty coupons based on a very complicated formula involving age, height, weight and shoe size.

Children's clothes were cheaper in coupon terms than those of adults; for instance, in 1942, a woman's woollen dress was eleven coupons, a girl's eight, an adult's fully-lined woollen overcoat eighteen coupons, a child's eleven. These examples also give an idea of how tight clothes rationing was: if a woman were to buy a woollen dress and overcoat, totalling twenty-nine coupons, almost half her annual allocation would be used up.

Far left: With clothes rationing, making your own became the order of the day. Knitting was very popular, as shown by this boy's hand-knitted windcheater.

Left: A teenage girl's hand-knitted sweater from one of the many knitting pattern books that were published at this time.

Of course, like every thing else, it got worse as the war went on. One year later the number of coupons was reduced to sixty for fourteen months, while all children up to seventeen got ten extra coupons. In spite of these extras, clothing children was a real headache: not only did they wear out their clothes much more quickly than adults, but they grew out of them as well. Working-class families had always handed down children's clothes, but for the middle classes this was a new experience. To cover the latter, the Women's Voluntary Services introduced children's shoe and clothing exchanges, where outgrown items could be exchanged. Then there was 'Make-do and Mend' – under this scheme women were encouraged to take apart old garments, remove the worn or torn parts and remake them into new clothes. Men's clothes, especially those of men off fighting the war, were especially targeted for this. A child's dress could be made from an old dinner jacket, a romper suit made from a pair of pyjama trousers, and so on.

Knitting was another way around rationing. New wool needed coupons, but once again, 'make-do and mend' meant finding old knitted garments, taking them down, washing the wool to get the kinks out, and knitting it into something new.

Right: 'Make-do and Mend' was the slogan for clothes, converting all sorts of things into clothes, such as this dressing gown made from an old blanket.

April-May 1944

Bedtime Story

A really warm dressing-gown for a tiny tot presents a problem for mother. But here's an idea—make one from a small blanket. If baby has outgrown his cot you might use his discarded cot blankets. With gay contrast bindings, it would look adorable and would keep baby warm as toast.

When washing woollens you'll have to take extra care now there's no Lux. Rinse carefully or undissolved soap may stick to fibres and make woollens harsh and matted.

Wartime Clothes Service by the **LUX** *News Scout*

LX 2820-122   LEVER BROTHERS, PORT SUNLIGHT, LIMITED

As many men were away with the forces, their clothes became a rich source of material for conversion into clothes for their wives or families. Here a plus-four suit becomes a hat and coat.

Below: New wool required coupons, but many people saved coupons by unravelling old knitted garments and re-using the wool, as is humorously shown in this postcard from the period.

From Daddy's Plus-Four Suit

A Warm Little Hat And Coat For The Three-Year-Old

My husband has given me permission to cut up his old plus-four suit to make something for my small son, aged three years. Do you think that it would be possible to make him a coat and leggings?
—Mrs. S. (Devon).

YOU will not be able to make leggings as well as a coat for your little boy, I am afraid. The jacket fronts of a plus-four suit will not be of much use owing to the pockets and the darts which shape it. However, you can make a neat overcoat and a hat, as shown in the illustration.

Cut the coat fronts from the back widths of the plus-fours, and use the front widths to cut the skirt back of the little coat with a stitched seam down the centre.

The yoke or bodice back for the coat and also the front facings can be cut from the back of the man's jacket. The small sleeves can—of course—be cut from the large ones, and there will

Bestway Pattern No. A.20,647. Price 1/-. (By post 1/1d.) Overseas 1/3d. The pattern is cut in sizes 2 and 3 years. Address orders to "Woman's Weekly" Paper Pattern Department, 21, Whitefriars Street, London E.C.4.

The old plus-four suit.

WOOL WITHOUT COUPONS GIRLS— EVERYBODY'S DOIN' IT NOW!

Knitting books abounded with patterns for children's clothes, not just for jumpers and scarves, but balaclava helmets, ties, socks and stockings, hats, and even underwear. Best remembered by many wartime children was the dreaded knitted swimming costume, which looked fine when dry, but took on a life of its own as soon as it got wet.

It wasn't always easy to find the amount of wool required for a particular item, so the old fashioned Fair Isle pattern was brought back; comprising a bit of this and a bit of that, it was perfect, and Fair Isle jumpers, hats, slippers, and just about anything else, became a common sight.

In 1943, the first red clothing books were issued, with variations for children and juniors; these would remain almost unchanged until clothes rationing ended in March 1949.

At the beginning of October 1941, a milk distribution scheme was brought in. Children under twelve months received 14 pints a week; expectant mothers and the under-sixes, 7 pints, and children from six to eighteen, half a pint a day. Once again the remainder was distributed among the rest, augmented by condensed milk supplemented from November by one tin a month of American evaporated milk. That month National Household (dried) milk was introduced, and a scheme for eggs; the same priority cases would receive four eggs for every one for the general public – this still meant that priority cases only got about one a week!

Many took to keeping their own chickens or even ducks in their garden; this was a job that was often done by the children of the family. There was one problem: if feeding humans was difficult, feeding animals could be a real headache. You could, of course, grow vegetables for feeding. The *Girls' Own Paper* recommended for hens Jerusalem artichokes, beet, carrots, potatoes, swedes, turnips, leeks, onions, and all sorts of winter greens. For rabbits, almost anything, especially hay, parsnips, beet, carrots, and kohlrabi.

In December 1941 the Vitamin Welfare scheme started. Babies, children, expectant and nursing mothers received orange juice and (less popularly) cod liver oil. Children under two were also issued with blackcurrant purée, while babies under six months received blackcurrant

Below left: Fair Isle was just the job for knitting using wool salvaged from old knitwear – you did not need the right amount of wool in one colour, but could use bits and pieces from several garments.

Below: Child's clothing ration book from 1943. As with food rationing, there were children's and junior clothing books containing extra coupons.

BESTWAY
LEAFLET 1681 3d.

FAIR ISLE BERETS
(SIZE 2 to 3 YEARS)
Each beret requires 1 oz. and oddments of 3-ply

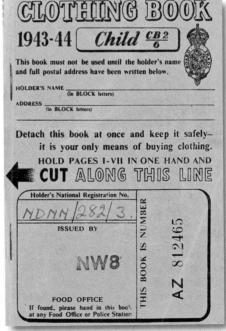

CLOTHING BOOK
1943-44 *Child* CB2/6

This book must not be used until the holder's name and full postal address have been written below.

HOLDER'S NAME _____ (in BLOCK letters)
ADDRESS _____ (in BLOCK letters)

Detach this book at once and keep it safely– it is your only means of buying clothing.

HOLD PAGES I-VII IN ONE HAND AND
CUT ALONG THIS LINE

Holder's National Registration No.
NDNN 282 3.
ISSUED BY
NW8
FOOD OFFICE
If found, please hand in this book at any Food Office or Police Station

THIS BOOK IS NUMBER
AZ 812465

Above: From December 1941, under the government's Welfare Scheme, children were entitled to concentrated orange juice, universally loved, and cod liver oil, almost as universally hated.

syrup instead of purée. The following April, the Vitamin and Milk schemes were joined together; only those entitled to free milk received welfare supplements free, everyone else had to pay 10d a bottle for cod liver oil (containing six weeks' supply) and 5d for orange juice (enough for two weeks). Charges were also made for blackcurrant purée and syrup.

The greatest blow to most children came on 26 July 1942 when sweet rationing was introduced in the form of 'personal points', and a 'Personal Ration Book' was issued. The ration was first set at 8 ounces a month, increasing in August to 16 ounces, then going back to 12 in October, where it remained. Confectionery manufacturers issued special ration-sized bars, but most children opted for sweets from the jars; tiny sweets known as 'hundreds and thousands' were popular, as they could be stretched a long way, as could the little orange and yellow 'pips'. Cough sweets were off ration, and children explored these and other alternatives. The Ministry of Food encouraged them to eat fruit, or better still, carrots, which they touted as a good, home-produced source of sugar and vitamin C.

The Government was aware that not all the extras aimed at children were actually consumed by them, often being shared amongst the family, so in that year the issue of the green ration book was changed from the under-sixes to those under five, as this fitted with school age, so that milk, cod liver oil and such items could be

CUT THEM INTO SLICES

and make the most of these two big-value chocolate coated candy bars

They are big not only in size but in delicious goodness, made from the very finest materials obtainable to-day (including separated milk and rich-with-energy glucose).

| MARS BAR | 2½D | STARRY WAY | 1½D |

The weekly sweet ration was enough for just one bar of chocolate. Mars suggested you slice up your bar to make it last!

issued at school. In July 1943 a blue Junior ration book was issued to children of six and over. In November 1943 a new drink, National Milk Cocoa, consisting mainly of milk, was introduced to provide nourishment to adolescents in industry who were therefore not covered by the school milk scheme. Employers could sell this to employees under eighteen for not more than 1d a half pint.

The 1943 blue 'Junior' food ration book, for school-aged children, who received extras such as milk.

The entry of America into the war in 1941 bought increasing numbers of US troops to Britain from 1942, bringing with them such luxuries as sweets, soap, nylons and comics. 'Got any Gum Chum?' was a popular song, based on the standard response of children to passing GIs.

HELPING WITH
THE WAR EFFORT

CHILDREN were encouraged to get involved with the war effort in many ways, the most common being collecting salvage and 'digging for victory'. Britain's dependence on imported raw materials and food was a weak spot, with Germany, through its U-boat wolf packs, attempting to starve it into submission.

Conservation of scarce raw materials became vital, and salvage drives sprang up with posters everywhere; the list of salvage material included metal, paper, silver paper, rubber, bones, rags, and left-over food for pigs.

Schools and youth groups organised salvage collections, often adding to the children's enthusiasm by turning them into competitions to see which school could collect the most paper, for example, or which Scout group the most scrap metal. The Women's Voluntary Service ran the 'Cog in the Wheel' scheme, whereby children received a badge for collecting a certain amount of salvage.

When not collecting salvage, you might 'do your bit' in the autumn by helping to bring in the harvest. Many youth organisations turned this work into a sort of holiday, camping on the farm (sometimes known as 'farmping') or, for younger children, travelling out for the day. There was also a Ministry of Agriculture scheme known as 'Lend a Hand on the Land'; usually restricted to older boys. Camping equipment was lent by the Ministry, while scouters' and teachers' wives, in cooperation with the WI and WVS, did the catering. In 1941, as part of the scheme, students from Oxford University taught secondary schoolboys how to drive tractors.

A variation of this was collecting the 'hedgerow harvest', where wild fruit, nuts, and so on, were picked to make the greatest use of wild food, or medicinal plants, such as sphagnum moss, foxgloves, deadly nightshade, coltsfoot, nettles, and especially rose hips, for which the WVS paid collectors 3d a pound!

Growing your own food, known as 'Dig for Victory', was another part of the war effort in which children could play a part, with schools, and Brownie and Guide groups keeping their own 'Victory Gardens' or even allotments, and local councils issuing certificates to successful growers.

Opposite: Older teenagers were encouraged to help with the harvest or haymaking, as shown here. Not only was it useful to the country, it was also a good holiday. (IWM TR 1300)

Government poster, 'The Three Salvageers': Rags, Bones and Paper. Collecting salvage was a job that could be done by children, and they did so with a will.

THE THREE SALVAGEERS.

Below right: Girl Guides collecting salvage. Children's organisations such as the Guides played an important part in the war effort through such events as salvage drives.

Below: With so many men in the forces, helping gather in the all-important harvest was yet another vital job that children were encouraged to take part in.

There were many local and national youth organisations in existence in the years leading up to the war. These geared up to play an active role on the home front, and were joined by newly formed groups who sprang up during the course of the war. They played such an important role that, at the end of 1941, it became compulsory for all those aged between 16 and 18, who were not already members of a recognised youth organisation, to join one.

It would be impossible in the space available here to document the activities of all the youth organisations, so a flavour of their contribution to the war effort will be given by looking at some of the bigger organisations.

These Guides are collecting sphagnum moss, to be used in making medicines. It was crucial that Britain made full use of all its natural resources.

GIRL GUIDES AND BROWNIES

In 1939 there were over half a million Girl Guides in the United Kingdom. As with many youth organisations, war at first brought problems for the guides, as many guiders joined the women's auxiliary forces, leaving many groups leaderless. This became known as the time of the patrol leaders, with the running of many groups devolving onto them.

Guides and Brownies began collecting salvage and started company allotments from the very start of the war, even before the national campaigns for these things were launched. Their early waste paper collections were sold

Guides displaying the potato harvest from their allotment. 'Digging for victory' was another vital task in which the youth of Britain could play its part.

Right: Brownie
uniform from
1939. As the
war went on and
clothes rationing
was introduced,
the uniform
codes of youth
organisations
became less strict.

Far right: Two
young wartime
Girl Guides in
full uniform.
(IWM TR 1863)

to paper manufacturers and the money used to buy wool, which the girls knitted into 'services comforts' – scarves, balaclava helmets, pullovers and so on – for the troops. In May 1940, there was a National Guide Gift Week, during which they raised money by giving up a week's pocket money. This aimed to buy two air ambulances and a lifeboat. Altogether £50,000 was raised, a huge amount then, enough to meet their target, with enough left over to pay for mobile canteens and rest huts which the YMCA would run for the troops.

Even young
children could 'do
their bit' for the
war effort. Here
Brownies are
working on
their allotment.

Early on Guides and Rangers took part in the distribution and fitting of children's gas masks, while some helped with painting kerbstones white. They assisted with evacuation, supplying food and drinks to the evacuee trains, and working as reception teams, meeting the evacuees at their destinations.

Later they helped in hospitals, first aid posts, maternity hospitals, and military convalescent homes. Here they rolled bandages, made beds, cleaned, served tea, helped prepare and serve meals, and talked to patients.

Others put their camping skills to work, giving public demonstrations of 'Blitz cooking' at the request of the Ministry of Food. This involved demonstrating how to cook over an open fire, or how to build an emergency oven, in blitzed areas where the gas and electricity had been cut off by bombing. Ranger Guides received training from wardens in putting out incendiary bombs, and about poison gas; they were also given pre-service training under the title of the Home Emergency Service.

The Guide Association issued a War Service badge consisting of a gold embroidered crown on a navy blue background. A separate strip showing the year was awarded for every year in which a Guide carried out war service.

SCOUTS AND WOLF CUBS

A plan to use Scouts as part of ARP had been worked out early in 1939. This involved Scouts and Cubs being attached to wardens' posts, to be used as runners, but in October 1939 they were withdrawn when it was realised that this would be far too dangerous for such young boys. Later older Scouts were used as messengers for the ARP, Police and Fire services, and the Home Guard. Bill Stern remembers 'working every evening after school as a LDV

Two young Police Auxiliary Messengers. Running messages for the civilian services (Police, Fire Brigade and Civil Defence) was yet another way in which youngsters could help out.

Wolf Cubs, Scouts and Sea Scouts collecting salvage. (IWM TR 2132)

War Service Scouts armband worn by older scouts who had passed a series of tests including signalling, first aid, unarmed combat and ARP work.

(Local Defence Volunteer, later called the Home Guard) messenger. 'I clocked up over 150 evenings cycling around the district with messages providing LDVs with their forthcoming duty rosters. We did our message taking regularly for four nights each week, in uniform, after school, on bicycles in all weathers.'

Scouts were trained in civil defence and first aid, they formed fire-watching parties, and senior Scouts were attached to hospitals where they worked as messengers, orderlies and telephonists. One of their main wartime jobs was erecting Anderson and Morrison shelters: householders unable to erect the shelters themselves would contact the council, who would pass their names on to the local Scouts. Roy Harris was a Wolf Cub in Bexleyheath Kent: 'I can shut my eyes now and see the house owner's face when 12 or 14 boys with a leader and an adult from the company came into the house to erect the shelter.' Another national service job was playing the part of casualties, or gas victims, in civil defence exercises, and being bandaged or decontaminated by ARP personnel.

A National Service cloth badge was introduced in February 1939. This was a red cloth rectangle with a gold embroidered crown in the middle, flanked by the letters 'NS', also in gold, worn on the left breast of the uniform. To gain the badge a Scout had to demonstrate an ability to write and carry messages, special knowledge of the local area, and of how to deal with panic and keep discipline. They also had to perform some form of national service. Bill Stern earned his badge from his Home Guard messenger work. 'Our Scout Master set a target of erecting 12 shelters to qualify for a National Service Badge and some of the troop were quite envious when I joined already wearing one from my time at Wokingham!'

60,000 scouts were awarded the Scout National Service Badge; later, there was a Civil Defence Proficiency Badge, and the Scout War Service Badge. The latter entailed signalling, first aid, unarmed combat, mapping, observation, weapons training, and ARP work. Early in 1942, as a response to the compulsory registration of sixteen-year-olds, War Service Scout Patrols were set up to work with the ARP or Home Guard. These patrols consisted of six to eight boys, one being the patrol leader. Clothes rationing meant that uniforms for new members were difficult to obtain and non-Scouts who joined these patrols were authorised to wear ordinary clothes with a Scout War Service armlet and the Scout lapel badge.

THE RED CROSS AND ST JOHN AMBULANCE BRIGADE

Children between the ages of twelve and fifteen could join the Red Cross Cadets, transferring to the Youth Detachment at fifteen where they could remain until they were twenty, or become full members of the Red Cross at sixteen if they passed examinations in first aid and, for girls, home nursing.

Training included first aid, home nursing, hygiene, cooking and infant welfare, handicrafts, ARP training, physical exercises and folk dancing. Many members worked part-time in hospitals relieving nurses (cleaning and feeding patients, bandaging and stitching), helping in hospital libraries, canteens and elsewhere, or in First Aid Posts. Others assisted in the Blood Transfusion Service, in children's nurseries, and similar duties. Very similar work was carried out by the Cadet Nursing Division of the St John Ambulance Brigade.

Most of the other existing youth groups carried out similar tasks, emphasising their own particular strengths or beliefs. There were, of course, those who already had a military purpose: the Army Cadets, one of the oldest youth organisations; the Air Training Corps, set up as the Air Defence Cadet Corps in the spring of 1938; and the Sea Cadets. All three groups provided

NCOs of the Air Training Corps being inspected.

Sea Cadets, with their band, on parade in Streatham.

initial service training for boys, including the use of arms, with the aim of providing peacetime recruits. In wartime many of their members, due to this initial training, would go on to become officers or NCOs when called up.

But these were for boys only — one of the features of the Second World War was the rise of the women's auxiliary services, the ATS, the MTC, the WAAFS, and the Wrens, amongst others. It was only natural then that there would be girls' pre-service units set up, along the lines of the boys' units.

THE WOMEN'S JUNIOR AIR CORPS

First was the Women's Junior Air Corps, set up in Worthing soon after war broke out under the name of the Women's Air Cadet Corps, the name being changed in February 1940. Its aim was to equip girls from fourteen to eighteen years old to play a part in the national effort. They received instruction in physical training, games, first aid, and morse, plus optional courses in anti-aircraft duties, radio location, signals, driving, engineering and electrical work, or clerical and office duties. There were also WJAC bands, which took part in church and other large parades.

Their first uniform consisted of a white or light blue blouse, a blue or black skirt, tie, and grey side cap; later a grey jacket and skirt were added. In its first eighteen months six squadrons were formed, nine months later that had risen to forty, and over two hundred six months later. In August 1942 the Government ordered a halt on the formation of any new WJAC units, although those already in existence were allowed to remain.

THE GIRLS' TRAINING CORPS

In April 1941 came the Girls' Training Corps, first formed in Croydon. Unlike the WJAC with its leanings towards the WAAF, the purpose of the GTC was to prepare girls between fourteen and eighteen for all branches of the women's services. Many of the early units were set up in boarding schools such as Cheltenham Ladies' College.

A report by the Streatham company of the Girls' Training Corps described their training:

> Lectures and practical demonstrations have been held in all basic subjects – first aid, home nursing, fire-fighting and gas, dispatch carrying, handywomen's course, physical training and drill. By arrangement with the London County Council, classes have been held in leatherwork, make-do and mend, motor engineering and ballroom dancing. Private instructors have given courses in Morse, typing, shorthand, and radio engineering, whilst through the kindness of the London Computator Corporation Ltd those girls who wished to do so have been able to learn the intricacies of computator operation.

Women's Junior Air Corps band on parade. Youth organisations played a central part in all wartime parades during War Weapons Week and other such local events.

Members of the Girls' Training Corps (GTC) doing physical training. Keeping fit was one of the central activities of wartime youth groups.

Below: Advertisement from September 1942 for books for the GTC and others. The list gives an insight into the sort of subjects in which the Corps specialised.

Because it was formed just before clothes rationing was introduced, the uniform was simple, being a skirt, blouse, tie and dark blue side cap. The GTC had its own parade song, which began:

We're here to help our country
Shoulder her heavy load.
This is the way to victory,
This is the surest road.

Chorus
We are cadets of the GTC
Our youth to our country we bring.
Willing and ready we'll always be
To serve our God and our King.

Members of the Girls' Naval Training Corps on Parade. Formed in 1942, after clothes rationing was introduced, their uniform, like that of the GTC, was deliberately kept simple.

THE GIRLS' NAVAL TRAINING CORPS

In March 1942 the Girls' Naval Training Corps was formed for girls from sixteen to eighteen, 'though some who are in reserved jobs are a little older'. The first unit was formed at Bromley in Kent, followed by four others, including Bournemouth, Poole and Dagenham.

Girls were taught the same seamanship skills as the Sea Cadet Corps, including knots and splices, chart work, warship recognition, swimming, the handling of boats and the rule of the road at sea. Their uniform, post-rationing, was simple: navy skirt, plain white blouse, black tie with naval crown badge, white lanyard and a man o'war cap (this was a sailor's round hat, costing 3s. 3d each) with the gold initials 'GNTC' on the ribbon.

From August 1942, in order to halt the proliferation of new groups, it was decided by the Board of Education to merge the various specialised training corps into the Girls' Training Corps. Any new units raised were to be GTC companies, although existing units could keep their older titles.

Below: Poem from the *Tiptop* comic of January 1943. *Tiptop* was a comic for younger children, who could still help out with such things as salvage collection.

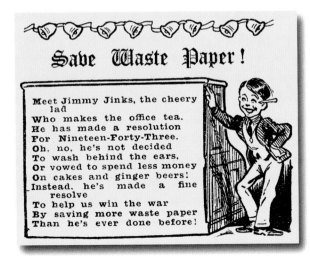

Save Waste Paper!

Meet Jimmy Jinks, the cheery lad
Who makes the office tea.
He has made a resolution
For Nineteen-Forty-Three.
Oh, no, he's not decided
To wash behind the ears,
Or vowed to spend less money
On cakes and ginger beers!
Instead, he's made a fine resolve
To help us win the war
By saving more waste paper
Than he's ever done before!

SPARE TIME

AT FIRST, there was no shortage of toys in the shops, although there was a definite change of emphasis: toys reflected the war. Derek Lambert, quoted in *The Home Front*, speaks of Christmas 1939: 'Toy shops were filled with khaki howitzers, scale models of warships, tin helmets, marbles, fret-saws, biplanes to be made from balsa wood and crashed in the back garden, guns and more guns.' Other popular presents that year were replica service uniforms, so that boys could wear the same RAF, Army, or Navy uniform as their father or brother; for girls there was always a nurse's uniform (the women's services – ATS, WRNS, WAAF and Land Army – had not seized the public imagination), or a doll dressed in uniform.

By Christmas 1940, the emphasis had changed: the Blitz had arrived and presents were more likely to be something to keep the children occupied in the air raid shelter. Books were popular, as were card games, puzzles and board games.

As the war dragged on, more and more toy manufacturers went over to munitions, and the supply of raw materials to non-war-related production was drastically cut back. In January 1942, the manufacture of metal toys was prohibited, while the Ministry of Supply, in a response to shortages, prohibited the manufacture of many rubber goods, including children's balloons. By Christmas that year almost the only toys to be found in the shops were highly priced secondhand ones, often in far from perfect condition. Once again, the Women's Voluntary Services provided a solution in the form of toy exchanges.

For most people the answer was to make their own toys, though here again, shortages of raw materials caused problems. 'Make-do and mend' helped: knitted toys abounded, while stuffed sheep were made from old towels, bears from the fake fur collar of an old coat, and pigs from old vests. The Blitz itself provided a great deal of scrap wood for making toys, with off-duty ARP workers and firemen making toys for hospitals and orphanages, while factory workers would spend their breaks making toys from left-over pieces of aluminium or perspex.

Opposite: Children's toys, December 1940, including aircraft, tanks, and barrage balloons. Early wartime toys were very war-oriented.

Right: Love-a-duck pattern. As the war went on more and more toys were home-made, often from patterns such as this.

Below left: Meccano from spring 1940. Within a year toys would almost disappear from the shops, as factories went over to war work.

Below right: The cover of the *Boy's Own Paper*, July 1940. Shortage of newsprint meant that comics became smaller and thinner as the war progressed, but were still eagerly swapped in the playground.

Comics and books could still be bought in shops, although, like newspapers, comics shrank, both in size and in the number of pages. There were many favourites, including, for younger children, *Beano*, *Dandy*, *Jingles*, *Film Fun* and *Radio Fun*, and for those in their teens, *Champion*, the *Girl's Own Paper* and the *Boy's Own Paper*. These would be read and re-read, then swapped in the playground. With the arrival of 'the Yanks' in 1942, came American comic books, lavish compared with the austere British versions, and highly prized in swapping circles.

Before the war cigarette cards were the big craze, collecting and swapping film stars, football and cricket players, cars, ships and aeroplanes, and in 1938, an ARP set with instructions on putting out incendiary bombs and so on. Sadly, paper shortages killed off the cigarette card at the beginning of the war, but these were soon replaced with something even more exciting – shrapnel. Spent bullet cases, incendiary bomb fins, anti-aircraft shell noses, and splinters from bombs and shells were eagerly sought. As soon as the all-clear sounded, children would scurry from the shelters to scour the area for prized pieces; a still warm piece of shell or bomb was regarded as a real find. Once again swapping was rife, and some enterprising groups mounted

exhibitions of their combined shrapnel collections, charging an entrance fee that went towards the local Spitfire Fund. Not all such shrapnel was harmless, and the wardens and police were kept busy relieving indignant youngsters of such prized finds as unexploded incendiary bombs.

Especially deadly was the butterfly bomb; this was roughly the size of a tin of beans, with a set of four vanes that gave it its name. The butterfly bomb was a vicious anti-personnel bomb that would explode at the slightest touch.

The German landmine or parachute mine was one bomb-related item that rarely fell into the hands of children. It was dropped, as its second name suggests, on a green silk parachute. At a time of clothes shortages the parachutes would be snapped up by women to be made into blouses, wedding dresses, or more often into underwear.

Television was around in 1939, although sets were very expensive, and the service very poor by today's standards. There was one channel only, in black and white, and just three hours' broadcasting a day, from six to nine o'clock in the evenings. However, even that disappeared at the beginning of September 1939, as broadcasting ceased 'for the duration'.

The 'wireless', as radio was then called, became, for the vast majority, the centre of home entertainment. Children listened to 'Children's Hour' with Uncle Mac, Larry the Lamb, and *Toytown*, while family favourites included *Garrison Theatre* with

A collection of shrapnel such as this would be the pride of many children during the Blitz.

'Blackout' board game. With advent of the real blackout, such board games were at a premium as families were confined at home, and later, in the air raid shelters.

51

Right: By November 1941, even the materials for making home-made toys were scarce. This sheep is cunningly made from an old white towel.

Far right: A model spitfire from July 1940. With the Battle of Britain just about to begin, any boy would have been proud of such a toy.

IN FULL FLIGHT !

FAST AND STABLE IN THE AIR
Produced by watch-precision machinery in the largest model aeroplane factory in the world by International Model Aircraft Limited. Obtainable at all good toyshops and stores

READY TO FLY 5'6 EACH
Write for details at other retailers

FROG
VICKERS-SUPERMARINE
SPITFIRE

Sole Concessionaires : LINES BROS. LTD., TRIANG WORKS, MORDEN ROAD, LONDON, S.W. 19

Jack Warner, *Bandwagon* with 'big-hearted Arthur' Askey and 'Stinker' Murdoch, and *Hi Gang* with Ben Lyons and Bebe Daniels. But the biggest of them all was *ITMA* (*It's That Man Again*), with Tommy Handley, Funf, Mrs Mopp, Colonel Chinstrap, and a whole crowd of characters, each with their own catchphrases.

When war broke out, the Government ordered all cinemas to be closed down, fearing high casualties should one be bombed. Within a few days, however, they were forced by public demand to reverse what had proved to be a catastrophe in terms of morale. People needed entertainment, and 'the pictures' were hugely popular. At first, many of the films were war inspired, such as *Target for Tonight*, and *One of Our Aircraft is Missing*, but far more popular were comedies. Top box-office star George Formby played a war-reserve

'ITMA' (It's That Man Again) was the most popular wireless programme of the war. Here are two of the show's stars, Mrs Mopp (Dorothy Summers) and 'That Man' himself, Tommy Handley.

policeman, an RAF recruit, a home guardsman, a sailor and many other characters in a string of war-time films. Will Hay starred in, amongst other films, *The Goose Steps Out*, while Tommy Trinder added light relief to *The Foreman Went to France*, and *The Bells Go Down*.

As with comics, the US brought a touch of (technicolour) glamour, with Disney bringing out *Dumbo*, *Bambi*, and the wonderful short, *Der Führer's Face* (featuring Donald Duck), while Popeye took on the Japanese

Imperial forces armed with just a tin of spinach. But the smash hit film of the war was *Gone With the Wind*.

Watching football was always an option, although teams lost many players to the forces, and the fixture list was radically altered to create area leagues in order to avoid fans having to travel. Other matches had an even more local feel – the

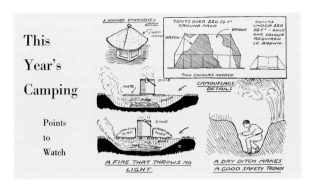

local ARP versus the Fire Brigade, and so on. These were often part of local National Savings programmes, including Spitfire Week, Salute the Soldier Week, War Weapons Week, and Warship Week, as part of which there would also be concerts, parades, fancy-dress competitions, sports events, demonstrations and dances. Similar events formed part of Holidays at Home Week, where a programme of local events encouraged people not to go away for their summer holidays.

'Camping in Wartime', from the *Boy's Own Paper* of July 1940, showing how to avoid breaking the blackout rules, camouflage your tent, and how to be ready for air attack.

The reality of a beach holiday in summer 1940 when invasion was expected. There was barbed wire and probably mines on the beach, while much of the south and east coasts were restricted areas, open only to locals.

53

EPILOGUE

O N 8 May 1945, VE Day, the war in Europe finally came to an end. Over the next few days Britain celebrated, and at the centre of the celebrations were the children: at street parties, dances, sports and fancy-dress competitions, and at small, family get-togethers the children were usually the focus of events.

Special food and drink, long put by for the event, were brought out. That night sights unseen since 1939 were revealed, street lights were switched on and public buildings were lit up by the searchlights which had combed the skies for enemy bombers. Bonfires blazed everywhere and fireworks filled the sky.

Then on 15 August came VJ Day. The Second World War was over, and, in a repeat of VE Day, Britain celebrated. Yet, for many, this only marked the end of hostilities – the scars would take a lot longer to heal. The troops began to return; long-absent fathers came home, having been seen only for two or three odd weeks' leave in the last six years. This long-awaited event far too often became a heartbreak, as young children shrank away from the 'stranger' who came between them and their mother. In other cases it was the children who returned as strangers, from evacuation, and they were not always welcomed with open arms. Families and their relationships had to be rebuilt, and this would often take months, if not years.

Many other things had to be rebuilt, including houses, shops and schools destroyed by the bombs and the V-weapons. This too would take a long time, but for the children the ruins became their playgrounds.

For many, the most disappointing thing was that rationing continued. Food, clothes, and (especially hard for the children) sweets would continue 'on the ration' for several more years. This, and many of the other side-effects of war – psychological scars, nightmares, disrupted education, fractured families and the deaths of family and friends – would take even longer to put right, especially for the children, many of whom could not remember what peace was like.

Opposite:
VE Day party.
Germany has
surrendered and
Britain rejoices,
but for many the
scars of war would
take a long time
to heal.

INDEX